WE DON'T KNOW HOW TO NOT FIGHT

A SCREENPLAY BY

FELICIA GUY-LYNCH

WE DON'T KNOW HOW TO NOT FIGHT

Dedication
To all the warriors

WE DON'T KNOW HOW TO NOT FIGHT

WE DON'T KNOW HOW TO NOT FIGHT

Over purple we hear music. Superimpose: **TODAY.**

> KIZZY (V.O.)
> Girl…

> FATIMA (V.O.)
> …What's up?

> KIZZY (V.O.)
> I worry about Desta sometimes…

CRANE SHOT TO FIND:

1 EXT. CREEK PATHWAY - EVENING

FATIMA and KIZZY are walking on the pathway. They look at one another then walk closer to their discovery. A feeling starts to come over them. They can feel it in their gut. FATIMA screams, KIZZY looks at FATIMA. WE FADE PURPLE. Superimpose: YESTERDAY.

FADE IN:

2 INT. INTERVIEW ROOM - MORNING

YASMIN is nervous for her job interview. The White man that interviews her comes onto her. She kicks him in the balls then runs.

3 EXT. STREET CORNER - NIGHT

YASMIN and DESTA wait anxiously for another customer. They look like the typical prostitutes.

WE DON'T KNOW HOW TO NOT FIGHT

WE DON'T KNOW HOW TO NOT FIGHT

4 INT. CLOTHING STORE - AFTERNOON

KIZZY
I'm getting tired of her.

FATIMA
Tired of who?

KIZZY
Never mind.

FATIMA
Why not just speak your mind?

KIZZY
Because I still have some hope.

5 INT. HOUSE - MORNING

MR. and MRS. SOLARIN leave their country in pursuit of a better life. It was MRS. SOLARIN'S idea for the new endeavour.

6 EXT. HOUSE - AFTERNOON

A *For Sale* sign goes up while MR. and MRS. SOLARIN pack the essentials in the taxi van to go to their next destination.

7 EXT. SKY - MORNING

Plans descends onto the horizon.

7

WE DON'T KNOW HOW TO NOT FIGHT

8 INT. APARTMENT - EVENING

MR. and MRS. SOLARIN are unpacking boxes. Superimpose: **2 MONTHS LATER.**

MONTAGE TO:

MR. SOLARIN has alcohol in his hand, looking spaced out. MRS. SOLARIN is crying in the corner with a black eye. Baby boy crying.

9 EXT. STREET CORNER - NIGHT

YASMIN and DESTA are prostituting. Wearing a different outfit.

10 INT. APARTMENT - NIGHT

MONTAGE TO:

MRS. SOLARIN brings a hot plate of food to MR. SOLARIN. MR. SOLARIN hits the plate out of her hand. She bends down to clean it. He gives her an intense stare.

11 EXT. STREET CORNER - NIGHT

YASMIN fights off a man wanting more than he's willing to pay for. She kicks him in the crutches and gets away. She always seems to be running away form a predator.

WE DON'T KNOW HOW TO NOT FIGHT

12 EXT. DARK ALLEY WAY - NIGHT

YASMIN begins to break down after running for an extended period of time.

13 EXT. STREET CORNER - NIGHT

DESTA is continuing the prostitution. This time she's alone.

14 INT. BEDROOM - NIGHT

YASMIN is at home studying but wonders about the safety of DESTA.

15 INT. KITCHEN - MORNING

FATIMA and KIZZY are in the kitchen preparing food.

'Mom' appears on FATIMA'S phone screen as an incoming call.

KIZZY
(into phone)

Hi Mom. No, Desta's not here... Mom... I'm tired of having to go look for her... She doesn't listen to me... No... You know what? I'm not arguing with you over her. She's grown now. We'll talk later Mom. I love you.

She ends the conversation. She nods her head and FATIMA consoles her.

WE DON'T KNOW HOW TO NOT FIGHT

16 INT. CLASSROOM - MORNING

YASMIN receives a 'D' on her latest assignment. She looks very disappointed.

17 EXT. STREET CORNER - NIGHT

YASMIN grabs on DESTA'S arm to show her she doesn't need to prostitute anymore. DESTA goes in one of the customer's vehicle. YASMIN stands there, looking defeated and walks in the opposite direction of the car taking off.

18 INT. APARTMENT - NIGHT

MRS. SOLARIN holds her baby with a backpack and a handbag as tears stream down her face. MR. SOLARIN is passed out on the couch with an empty bottle in his hand.

19 INT. CLASSROOM - MORNING

YASMIN receives a 'C' on her latest assignment. She nods her head to celebrate her improvement.

20 INT. RUTH'S HOUSE - MORNING

KIZZY observes the puffers on the kitchen table. She places her belongings on the table and steps deeper into the house. She sees RUTH sitting in the living room, a woman in her 60's, coughing up a storm. She steps into the living room, kneels down beside her and holds her hand.

WE DON'T KNOW HOW TO NOT FIGHT

> RUTH
> Did you find your sister?

> KIZZY
> No.

> RUTH
> Tell her to come home. She can't manage it out there all
> by herself.

And she coughs again. KIZZY kisses her on the cheek
and looks at her with concern.

21 INT. FATIMA'S CAR - MOMENTS LATER

KIZZY approaches and jumps in.

> FATIMA
> Is Mommy ok?

> KIZZY
> Yup.

KIZZY gives her a look as a car wipes the frame…

22 EXT. DARK ALLEY WAY - NIGHT

MRS. SOLARIN is walking with her baby.

23 INT. CLASSROOM - MORNING

YASMIN receives an 'A' on her latest assignment. She
smiles at her improvement.

WE DON'T KNOW HOW TO NOT FIGHT

24 INT. FATIMA'S CAR - MORNING

KIZZY and FATIMA are in the car listening to music.

25 EXT. DARK ALLEY WAY - NIGHT

MRS. SOLARIN is sitting with her baby.

26 INT. BEDROOM - MORNING

YASMIN shows DESTA the mark on her assignment. DESTA is happy for her friend but a look of uncertainty soon follows. She doesn't know where she fits. She feels out of place.

27 INT. HOMELESS - NIGHT

MRS. SOLARIN is lying down with her baby. An incoming phone call shows up from BEN SOLARIN. She presses IGNORE. An incoming text comes from her husband saying, "I'm sorry I failed you both. I want another chance."

28 INT. FATIMA'S CAR - MORNING

FATIMA turns down the music.

FATIMA
I think you need to check up on your sister before it's too
late.

KIZZY just looks at FATIMA then looks away.

WE DON'T KNOW HOW TO NOT FIGHT

29 EXT. STREET CORNER - NIGHT

DESTA goes into MR. SOLARIN'S car.

30 INT. MR. SOLARIN'S CAR - NIGHT

MR. SOLARIN goes from kissing DESTA and having his hands around her neck to chocking her to death.

31 EXT. CREEK - MORNING

His mind going full speed, MR. SOLARIN gets out the driver seat, makes his way to open the passenger seat, drags DESTA out the creek. We focus on DESTA'S lifeless body as MR. SOLARIN walks past her body.

32 INT. MR. SOLARIN'S CAR - MORNING

MR. SOLARIN starts to break down, placing both hands on the steering wheel and head between his arms.

33 INT. POLICE STATION - MORNING

MR. SOLARIN walks toward the police station to turn himself in. He's a man full of regret, sorrow and hopelessness.

34 INT. INTERVIEW ROOM - MORNING

The white woman that interviews her shakes YASMIN'S hand.

WE DON'T KNOW HOW TO NOT FIGHT

WHITE WOMAN
You're hired. We'd love to have you on our team.

YASMIN is all smiles.

35 INT. RUTH'S HOUSE - MORNING

KIZZY observes RUTH lying down in the bedroom. She gets a garbage bag and starts picking up scraps from the ground.

36 EXT. SIDEWALK - MORNING

YASMIN is dialling DESTA'S number. She doesn't get her. She shrugs it off but still wonders about the whereabouts of her friend.

37 EXT. SIDEWALK - EVENING

FATIMA analyzes the hand and realizes it's DESTA'S hand. The ring on her hand gives it away.

38 INT. BEDROOM - MORNING

YASMIN receives an incoming call from KIZZY. She picks up. Conversation is in slow motion. YASMIN puts her hand over her mouth, drops the phone, then puts both her hands on her face.

WE DON'T KNOW HOW TO NOT FIGHT

39 INT. MORGUE - MORNING

YASMIN and KIZZY are standing in front of a gurney. The Male Coroner Tech flips back the sheet enough for them to see. YASMIN'S leg buckles, her mouth opens while KIZZY comforts her as tears fall down her face as well.

40 INT. GRAVEYARD - AFTERNOON

YASMIN drops flowers at DESTA'S grave side.

41 INT. APARTMENT - MORNING

MRS. SOLARIN is sitting on the edge of the bed with the lamp on, wearing her night gown, looking like she's deep in thought while she caresses the baby. She is trying to pick up the pieces from a broken marriage.

42 INT. PRISON CELL - MORNING

MR. SOLARIN grips the cell bars with both his hands while staring out; regretful.

43 EXT. SIDEWALK - EVENING

All that's left is a piece of the crime scene tape. KIZZY sits in the area close to where DESTA'S body was found. She then stares out; lost and in despair.

44 INT. CONVOCATION - MORNING

YASMIN is dressed in convocation attire. She holds the flowers in her hand while KIZZY takes a picture of YASMIN and RUTH smiling. The family is delighted for YASMIN's graduation.

THE END